Original title:
The Gentle Glow of Christmas Spirit

Copyright © 2024 Creative Arts Management OÜ
All rights reserved.

Author: Alexander Thornton
ISBN HARDBACK: 978-9916-94-034-1
ISBN PAPERBACK: 978-9916-94-035-8

A Celebration of Light and Love

Twinkling bulbs dance on the tree,
Elves tripping over their glee.
Cookies vanish, oh what a sight,
Rudolph snickers, it's quite the night.

Stockings stuffed to the brim,
With gifts galore, chances slim.
A cat in the hat, what a vision!
Presents toppled in a wild collision.

Hot cocoa spills on Granny's lap,
As kids play a merry little tap.
Snowmen smile with carrot noses,
While snowflakes dance like silly roses.

Laughter rings out, the joy is shared,
With playful teasing, no one's spared.
Mistletoe mishaps and funny sights,
As love and fun spark Christmas nights.

Beneath the Evergreen Canopy

Under trees so tall and grand,
Squirrels scurry, oh so planned.
Chasing shadows, bouncing round,
In their joy, pure bliss is found.

Lights are tangled, what a sight,
Elves are wrestling, what a fright!
Tinsel flying, laughter rings,
Joyful chaos that the season brings.

Frost-Kissed Hope

Snowflakes dance like tiny jesters,
In mittens warm, we are the testers.
Hot cocoa spills, we giggle loud,
As marshmallows float, we feel so proud.

Frosty noses, cheeks aglow,
Ice skating falls, it's part of the show.
Hope slips like ice beneath our feet,
But chuckles rise, oh what a treat!

Kindness Wrapped in Wonder

Kindness comes in quirky shapes,
Wrapped in colors, like sweet grapes.
Presents wobble, tip and sway,
Who knew gifts could dance and play?

Granny's fruitcake, oh dear me!
It's like a brick; it's quite the spree!
But laughter fills the room so wide,
Kindness, oh, our joyful guide.

A Lantern for Every Heart

Lanterns twinkle, a vibrant glow,
Warming hearts in chilly snow.
Santa's sleigh goes 'whoosh' and zoom,
With reindeer prancing near the room.

Giggles bubble in the night,
Mittens lost in sudden flight.
Every heart, a lantern bright,
Shining joy, a merry sight!

Starry Eyes and Silent Nights

Under twinkling stars we prance,
Wishing on a star, a silly chance.
Santa's reindeer fly too high,
Landing on roofs, oh my, oh my!

Snowballs thrown with all our might,
Laughter echoing through the night.
Cookie crumbs on noses gleam,
Who knew food could make us dream?

Laughter on the Wind

The wind carries giggles and cheer,
A snowman's hat we'll commandeer.
Frosty's nose laughs with delight,
As we dance under the moonlight.

Sleds racing down hills so steep,
Laughter brings the joy from sleep.
Hot cocoa spills from someone's cup,
We laugh till we can't get up!

Fireside Fables and Secrets

By the fire, tales run wild,
Of a sneaky elf who's just a child.
Marshmallows toast until they're brown,
One ends up wearing a chocolate crown!

A cat in a blanket, purring near,
Stealing all the warmth and cheer.
The ghost of Christmas past arrives,
With socks, mismatched, he high-fives!

Threads of Joy in Winter's Fabric

With needles clicking, crafts take shape,
A sweater hug, but what a scrape!
Yarn tangled, a colorful mess,
But laughter makes it so much less!

Gifts wrapped badly, all askew,
Each one marks a special cue.
A holiday mishap brings us cheer,
With giggles loud, it's best time of year!

Scent of Pine and Promise

Oh, the tree's a little crooked,
With ornaments that wobble.
Scent of pine and tangled lights,
   Creating quite the gobble.

Uncle Bob mistook the eggnog,
For the dog's bowl, oh what fun!
The dog is now the life of it,
   And Uncle Bob will surely run.

A Glow that Fills the Soul

Twinkling lights shine on the yard,
But one strand's now on the roof.
Best call the cat, our brave little guard,
She'll balance, or she'll go poof!

Cookies baked with love and flair,
Some burnt, but who's to tell?
Squishy faces, flour in hair,
Happy chaos, all is well.

Hushed Moments Beneath the Tree

Underneath the tree we laugh,
With wrapping paper flyin'.
Mom's got a present for the staff,
But it's just a big old pylon!

Whispers sneak past cookies crunch,
As we plot a little prank.
The cat just pounced, made a mighty lunch,
Now no one's brave as Tank!

Luminous Hearts in a Frosty World

Faces bright with snowball fight,
They mix adventure with delight.
Mom's hot cocoa spilled, oh dear!
And Grandma's sweater, stuck right here!

Luminous hearts, we play till night,
Snowmen frozen in their plight.
The carrot's gone; where could it be?
Turns out it's lunch for the doggie!

Candles Flicker in the Stillness

In the corner, wax men dance,
Chasing shadows, take a chance.
Jingle bells ring out a tune,
While snowflakes start to pirouette too.

Gingerbread folks start to prance,
Rolling dough with a clumsy stance.
They trip and fall, oh what a sight,
Baking fails become pure delight.

Mittens lost and socks askew,
Santa's sleigh needs a tune-up too.
Reindeer giggle, munching hay,
As the snowman shouts, 'No work today!'

So light a candle, let it sway,
Make the darkness laugh and play.
Sipping cocoa, feeling bright,
This festive chaos feels just right!

Wrapped in the Season's Embrace

Bows are tangled, ribbons stuck,
Unruly gifts, oh what bad luck!
A cat wraps round the Christmas tree,
As ornaments fall like confetti spree.

Cookies vanish at a brisk pace,
Santa's munchies leave no trace.
Frosted windows, laughter loud,
Within this chaos, we are proud.

With each twinkle lights may fight,
As bulbs flicker on the ceiling bright.
Mismatched socks and winter cheer,
All this joy is wrapped sincere.

So grab some tinsel, hang it high,
With joyful hearts, we say goodbye.
For every mishap brings a grin,
In this embrace, let joy begin!

The Heart's Soft Radiance

The tree's a beacon, oh so grand,
Yet cats think it's a jungle land.
Ornaments fall like leaves from trees,
While giggles echo on the breeze.

Hot cocoa spills on Grandma's lap,
She smiles wide without a gap.
With marshmallows floating like dreams,
The laughter flows in endless streams.

Secret Santa's gift's a shock,
A rubber chicken, oh what luck!
Each wrapped surprise brings silly glee,
In this delight, we all agree.

So raise a mug, let spirits soar,
With laughter ringing, who could ask for more?
In every blunder, joy's released,
In this soft light, our hearts are pleased!

Frosty Breath of Kindness

With icy breath, the winds do tease,
They swirl around like funny bees.
Snowmen waddle with silly grace,
Matching hats, a snowy face.

A child throws snow with joyful screams,
As snowballs fly in wild, wild dreams.
A frosty mug slips from a hand,
Hot chocolate spills like a sugar sand.

Sleds go crashing, laughter bright,
While hot dogs plop at a snowy fight.
In snow-clad parks, good times abound,
With friendly banter, cheer is found.

So keep your gloves on, let's be loud,
As fluffy flurries swirl around.
With frosty breath and hearts aglow,
In every giggle, love will show!

Glowing Hearts in the Frost

In a town so cold, no one dares,
We wear our socks, and mismatched pairs.
Snowmen wink with twinkling eyes,
As reindeers play hide-and-seek in the skies.

Carols sung in off-key cheer,
While Aunt Edna steals the last piece of beer.
Hot cocoa spills on sweater vests,
As we laugh at the siblings' crazy quests.

Festive Whispers Beneath the Stars

Under twinkling stars, we plot our fun,
Where Santa's sleigh was really a bun.
The cookies we baked, oh what a sight,
We'll munch and crunch till the morning light.

Elves with jingle bells waddle around,
Confetti snowflakes float to the ground.
The cat in lights, so proud and spry,
Merry mischief under the frosty sky.

Chasing Dreams in the Winter Air

With snowflakes stuck in our hair and hats,
We'll build a snow fort, then eat the spats.
Sledding down hills, oh what a thrill,
Just watch your cousin with the sad old chill!

Frosty footprints lead to mischief galore,
While snowball fights leave us wanting more.
The wind whispers secrets of cheer and fun,
As we chase holiday dreams, one by one.

Threads of Love, Warm and Bright

Sweaters knitted with love and care,
From Grandma's yarn to Uncle's glare.
Each stitch is a hug, silly but warm,
While pets hide under the cottony swarm.

The lights in the house do a dance and spin,
As we sip on eggnog with a cheeky grin.
Wrapped gifts tumble, not quite a surprise,
When they open a dog toy that squeaks and cries!

Holiday Hues and Whispers of Love

Bright lights twinkle, oh what a sight,
Santa's got a dance move, now isn't that right?
Elves in the kitchen, making a fuss,
Spilling hot cocoa, on the cat – what a plus!

Mistletoe hangs over a door with a chime,
Who knew Grandma could still keep the time?
With cookies on plates shaped like a star,
We'll munch 'til we're merry, then call it a car!

Echoes of Laughter in the Frost

Snowflakes flutter, like a sitcom's scene,
Buddy the Elf would say, 'Aren't we keen?'
Frosty's lost his hat, what a hilarious plight,
Chasing him down, giggling with fright.

Gifts piled high, wrapping paper confetti,
A cat in a box? Oh, isn't that petty?
We'll play some tunes, while we laugh and we cheer,
'Is this the year we try something near?'

Whispers of Winter Nights

The moon is bright, like a disco ball,
Neighbors sing carols, what a funny call!
Hot cider spills – oh, what a hot mess,
Sipping it down, feeling the stress.

Socks on the fire, what a grand sight,
Grandpa's snoring, it's quite a delight!
Yule logs burning with stories to tell,
Who knew winter nights could go so well?

Stardust on Frosted Windows

Golden star toppers wobble and sway,
Kids giggling outside, trying to play,
A snowman is dancing – or is it a tree?
Either way, it's a sight, don't you agree?

Ornaments dangling, caught in the breeze,
A dog with a tinsel that wraps 'round with ease.
Our hearts are aglow, full of playful cheer,
Let the laughter ring, for it's that time of year!

Candlelit Dreams on a Snowy Night

In shadows warm, the candles flicker,
While snowflakes dance, oh what a sticker!
The cat's a spy, plotting his prance,
As cookies crumble, we steal a glance.

Grandpa's stories, they never end,
Of reindeer games, and jesting friends.
A tree adorned with tinsel so bright,
While squirrels giggle at our delight.

We sip the cocoa, marshmallows afloat,
While Auntie hums a jolly note.
The lights do twinkle, but not my shirt,
One day I'll learn to avoid the spurt!

So here we gather, laughter's our creed,
With silly hats and a wild stampede.
Christmas joy, a goofy parade,
In this merry mess, our hearts never fade.

Soft Radiance of Togetherness

In cozy corners, we find our cheer,
With fuzzy socks and a friendly beer.
The kids are bouncing, the dog, a blur,
He'll eat the leftovers—what a fur stir!

Outside the world wears a frosty grin,
While inside, the giggles and chaos begin.
A dance-off breaks out; who's got the moves?
The truth is, none—yet we all improve!

The pie's been baked with too much spice,
One slice turns out just a tad too nice.
In laughter we choke, as faces turn red,
A little too merry, we retire to bed.

With joy we gather, gifts piled high,
A silly hat for the wrong guy.
In this warmth, all worries cease,
Wrapped in laughter, we find our peace.

Embraced by Frosty Skies

Bundled tight in our woolly attire,
Outside we play in a snowball choir.
With rosy cheeks and laughter loud,
Our antics could make an iceberg proud.

The snowman's belly begins to sag,
While dogs in boots are a comical drag.
Sleds tumble down in a woosh and a roll,
We'll blame the cocoa, or maybe the troll!

Hot chocolate spills down my dad's nice coat,
He acts now like it's a top-notch quote.
Moms roll their eyes, with a chuckle or two,
While dad keeps yelling, 'I still love you!'

Beneath the stars, our stories unwind,
Silly traditions, not always refined.
In frosty cheer, our hearts entwine,
Making each moment a sparkling line.

The Melody of Kind Hearts

With jingling bells and laughter's song,
We celebrate together, where we all belong.
Around the piano, we take our turns,
Not quite on key, but our spirit burns.

Auntie's no-noodles, a festive soup,
The flavors come together in a wobbly loop.
As forks go flying, and jokes are told,
Our family bond is a sight to behold.

Our sweaters are ugly, we wear them with pride,
Each stitch and each pattern, a mountain to hide.
Uncle Bob dances like he's lost his shoe,
Yet, in this madness, we find something true.

So lift your glass, toast the clumsiness here,
In flops and in blunders, we shout out with cheer.
With laughter and love, our kindness imparts,
A melody sweet, from our kind, silly hearts.

The Gift of Presence

Gather round, the tree stands tall,
With ornaments that bounce and fall.
A misplaced star on Grandma's head,
We giggle as she struts in red.

Cookies all around, they start to crumble,
While Uncle Bob gets lost in the jumble.
He thinks he's dancing, oh what a sight,
But really he's just dodging the light.

Joyful laughter echoes through the halls,
As someone trips and spills the balls.
In our hearts the warmth will glow,
We forgot the fruitcake, so let's just go!

Emblazoned Hearts in Winter's Chill

Snowflakes fall with a fluffy cheer,
While Dad prances in his new reindeer.
The pets in sweaters look quite absurd,
They give us smiles without a word.

Hot cocoa spills as we start to race,
Grandma yells, 'It's not a marathon, brace!'
But who can resist in the joyful spree,
When hot cocoa also means running free?

A snowman's face from an old garden pot,
With googly eyes and a nose that's not.
We laugh and cheer, our hearts alight,
In this chilly joy, there's always delight.

Reflections of Starlit Dreams

The stars twinkle like bright little lights,
As we gather 'round for harmless fights.
But who can win in a board game maze,
When Dad just cheats in so many ways?

A toast with soda, we clink and cheer,
It's time to kick the holiday gear.
With dad's bad puns and mom's bright smile,
We forget the fuss by holding the style.

Dancing in circles, we drop like flies,
Mom starts laughing till her tears dry.
In every giggle, a memory spun,
In starlit dreams, we meld into one.

The Quiet Joy of Shared Surprises

Whispers float through the chilly air,
As we plot gifts without a care.
Mom's still lost in her own little zone,
While we sneak past her, we're on our own.

Wrapped up in blankets and cookies too,
We shift and shuffle, what's coming new?
A puppy that peeks through the shiny bow,
Hiding away, oh what a show!

Uneaten turkey from last year's feast,
We smile and say, "To each their least!"
Finding joy in every surprise,
With laughter as bright as the winter skies.

A Canvas of Memories Untold

In the attic lies a treasure,
Old tinsel made of gold and leisure.
Grandma's dance with a cake in tow,
Frosting everywhere, oh what a show!

Uncle Fred tries to fit the tree,
Ends up tangled, oh what a spree!
Cats climbing high, dogs steal the scene,
Christmas chaos, a scrapbook routine.

A gift that's wrapped like it's from Mars,
Turns out to be a jar of jars.
Laughter echoes, spirits uplift,
These memories are the real gift.

So here's to laughter and a jolly toast,
To the crazy moments we cherish the most.
With mischief, love, and a little delight,
A canvas rich in festive light.

The Warmth of Family Gatherings

A long table, mismatched chairs,
With Auntie's casserole and Cousin's glares.
Someone forgot to check the bread,
We've got a rock, please don't be misled!

Kids on sugar, running with glee,
Grandpa's snoring; how can this be?
The dog's underfoot, a turkey brigade,
Two pies are missing, they can't evade!

Hot cocoa spills on Uncle Joe,
"Oops," says the kid, "Did you see that flow?"
We chuckle and laugh at the messy scene,
Happiness blooms, like a festive green.

With stories told and jokes galore,
Each belch and giggle we all adore.
This crazy gathering, better than gold,
In warmth and laughter, our hearts are bold.

Finding Peace in Candlelight

Candlelight flickers, shadows waltz,
Mom's selling fruitcake; we think it's a fault.
Whispers surround the midnight cheer,
What was that noise? Did Santa appear?

Socks on the floor for reindeer to wear,
Only to find them—what a funny affair!
A gingerbread house that needs some love,
With gumdrops falling, just like a dove.

The cat's eyeing that warm, shiny glow,
While we sip hot cider, watch the show.
A laugh from the kitchen, "That's not the wine!"
Just Aunt Martha's famous grape juice, oh so fine!

In this soft lighting, we find our peace,
And all the oddities seem to increase.
With chuckles and sighs, we softly unite,
In the warmth of these memories, so bright.

Murmurs of Comforting Whispers

In quiet corners, secrets unfold,
Like grandpa's stories, often retold.
What's that there, a shadowy wraith?
Oh wait, it's just the neighbor's dog's faith!

Mom's recipe, what could go wrong?
The burnt edges always sing a wrong song.
Yet between the bites, we find great delight,
Laughing together deep into the night.

By the fire, we plan pranks on the elf,
Who seems to be spying on our Christmas shelf.
But when morning breaks, all's forgiven pie,
Especially when gifts are piled high and nigh!

So we whisper wishes on this snowy night,
Creating a chorus of pure delight.
With cuddles and chaos, our hearts feel the cheer,
In these murmurs of love, we hold dear.

Serenade of Snowflakes

Snowflakes dance like they're in a spree,
Landing softly, a fluffy jubilee.
They twirl and spin with comical grace,
Creating a snowman with a silly face.

Children giggle, their cheeks turning red,
As snowballs fly and laughter is spread.
With noses all chilly, they come inside,
Hot cocoa awaits for the frosty ride.

Mittens and hats all mismatched and wild,
Outside they're warriors, indoors a child.
With marshmallows floating, they joke and they cheer,
As the snowflakes giggle and disappear.

So here's to the snows, the laughs in the fray,
In the wintery wonder where we love to play.
For snowflakes and kids, both are quite rare,
And the joy of the season we all want to share.

A Tapestry of Giving

Gift wrap battles, oh what a sight!
Scissors fly left and right in the fight.
With ribbons that tangle and tape that won't stick,
A present emerges, it's stretchy and thick.

Neighbors exchange cookies, all oddly designed,
Some shaped like llamas, others unlined.
The laughter erupts, as we all take a bite,
"Is this gingerbread or a cake gone awry tonight?"

We try on our sweaters, so horrible, bright,
The patterns provoke chuckles, oh what a sight!
With each goofy grin, we spread all the cheer,
In this web of silliness, joy draws us near.

So let's share our blunders, our gifts wrapped with care,
In this tapestry woven of laughter and flare.
For giving is fun, when it's wrapped up in glee,
Creating memories, just you and me.

Illuminated Paths of Compassion

Twinkling lights wrap around every tree,
Looking like fairies that just want to be.
Neighbors peer out from their windows with glee,
As dogs bark in chorus at the lights and debris!

A wreath on the door swings open with cheer,
As visitors wander, shy of good beer.
"Hey look at your outfit!" they shout in delight,
All the while fretting it's not very bright.

Compassion is kind as we trip on the rug,
Spilling our snacks, giving each other a hug.
With laughter in surplus, we gather around,
To swap silly stories, our joy knows no bound.

So forge these warm trails, where folly collides,
With lights all aglow, and laughter that glides.
Paths of connection, bright warmth from the heart,
In this season of kindness, let's never part.

The Magic of Shared Moments

Gathering 'round for a feast and a cheer,
A table of chaos, that's what we hold dear.
With Grandma's strange dish that jiggles like joy,
Oh, what a spectacle, mismatched for a boy!

Pinecone decor that looks like a beast,
We can't help but giggle; it's not a feast.
Mom sighs in relief as the chaos unfolds,
While Dad takes a nap with "stories" retold.

Each clumsy handshake and awkward exchange,
Add charm to our moments that feel a bit strange.
From cousins that bicker to Grandma's "what's new?",
These jumbled connections just make us feel true.

So here's to the laughter, the memories spry,
In moments shared under the festive sky.
Where magic blooms in each quirky delight,
And joy is the secret that makes our hearts light.

Echoing Laughter Amidst the Snow

Snowflakes dance like clumsy sprites,
Hats fly off in snowy fights.
Hot cocoa spills, what a sight,
Laughter echoes through the night.

Snowmen wobble, noses askew,
They can't stand a chance with you.
A snowball flies with all your might,
We giggle at our frosty plight.

Sleds zoom by in joyful haste,
Hot chocolate, oh, what a taste!
But when you slip, just take the fall,
And join in the fun, laughing all!

As stars above begin to shine,
We jest and play, a sweet design.
In winter's chill, our hearts feel warm,
Together we create the charm.

The Warmth of Kindred Spirits

Gather round the glowing fire,
Tell tales of mischief, never tire.
We roast marshmallows 'til they burn,
While plotting pranks for next year's turn.

Scarves wrapped tight, and mittens misplaced,
We trip on ice with joyful haste.
Each little mishap, a source of glee,
As we burst out laughing, oh, can't you see?

We sip our drinks, all sticky sweet,
With cookies made by tiny feet.
Yet every bite brings giggles forth,
'Cause none of us can tell their worth.

Through jingle bells that ring so bright,
We dance like fools in soft moonlight.
The warmth of love, it fuels our cheer,
While laughter binds us, year after year.

Nights of Abundant Wishes

Under twinkling lights adorned with care,
We hang cookies, hoping bears will share.
Yet when it's cut, the taste's a shock,
Who knew flour could feel like rock?

Silent night with whispers loud,
Under soft blankets, we gather proud.
We dream of gifts that make us grin,
But wake up to socks and a rubber chin.

Wishing on stars, we scream with joy,
For legos, dolls, or just a toy.
Yet what arrives may just bemuse,
Like endless pairs of polka dot shoes.

Though we dream of snowmen built so tall,
We find ourselves in our neighbor's brawl.
A night full of wishes and laughter's flare,
Unwrap the smile, for love's everywhere!

Unwrapped Joy Beneath the Tree

Presents piled beneath the pine,
Who can resist that sparkling shine?
Rip the paper, oh what a mess,
A cat hides in every crumpled dress.

Tinsel tangled, oh what a sight,
Looks like the tree got into a fight.
As we giggle at the diamond stray,
We laugh, what else can we say?

With every gift, a story told,
Of mischief's plans that surely unfold.
We dance with joy, wrapped in delight,
Beneath mistletoe, all feels just right.

As the day fades with sparkly cheer,
Our hearts are light, our smiles sincere.
For in each laugh, a treasure found,
Unwrapped joy, it's all around.

A Tapestry Woven in Cheer

In the hall, there's a tree so bright,
With ornaments that are out of sight,
Dad's stuck up there, trying to reach,
While mom just laughs and hands him a peach.

The cat's in the lights, what a sight to see,
Dancing like a furry Christmas tree,
Grandma's baking cookies, oh what a smell,
But dad's snuck one; he's under the spell!

Uncle Joe's sweater is a crime on its own,
A mix of colors that have never been shown,
We giggle and tease, it's all in good fun,
He wears it with pride, and we're never done.

Outside there's snow, all fluffy and white,
No chance for a snowball fight tonight,
We'll roll a snowman, with a nose made of cheese,
And laugh 'til we cry, as we giggle with ease.

Twinkling Stars Above Our Heads

The stars are out, they twinkle so bright,
Like holiday lights in the still of night,
We squint and we point at the ones in our way,
'Is that a star? Or a plane gone astray?'

A snowman looks on with a carrot for nose,
Wearing dad's old hat that he claimed as his clothes,
But little Timmy, with a prank to deploy,
Just swapped the hat for his best pirate toy.

The trees sway gently, in rhythm, they sway,
While squirrels steal decorations, what a display!
With laughter and joy, the evening goes on,
Our faces aglow with each silly yawn.

A carol we sing, all off-key and loud,
Like a choir of cats, we should feel quite proud,
Yet the joy is a gift that we share with a grin,
In this cozy moment, where laughter begins.

Mistletoe and Memories

Under the mistletoe, we meet with a grin,
A peck on the cheek, then the family joins in,
But cousin Ben leaps in to steal the sweet kiss,
So we wrestle him down, oh what a giant mess!

Grandma recalls tales that we know all too well,
Of the time when aunt Sue made the kitchen smell,
With ham gone rogue and a fire in the pan,
Now we barely can breathe through our giggles and spans.

The eggnog is flowing, be careful, my friend,
Last year they tried spiking, oh what a trend,
And uncle Doug danced like a chicken gone wild,
That memory keeps us laughing like a child.

Reminders of laughter coat each holiday scene,
With mishaps and stories, our hearts burst at the seam,
So here's to the family, both silly and dear,
With mistletoe magic, we'll cherish each year.

The Warmth Beneath the Snow

Beneath the cold snow, a glow starts to rise,
From cocoa to laughter, it warms all our pies,
With marshmallows floating, cheer up our mugs,
Dad's secret recipe, now that's really snug.

The raccoon Cletus has found a fine prize,
A stash of old cookies, oh how he flies,
We chase him around, but he's nimble and spry,
While giggling we watch, as he waves us goodbye.

In the corner, the lights flicker bright,
We join hands and dance; oh, what a sight!
With the kitten who pounces and stumbles with glee,
This evening of joy is where we long to be.

So here's to the warmth that we all hold so tight,
As we laugh and we bake through the chilly old night,
With snows that may cover, our spirits will soar,
In the glow of our hearts, who could ask for more?

Love Letters in the Snow

In frosty air, my hands write fast,
With mittens on, I hardly grasp.
I penned a note, but it did fly,
Caught by a squirrel who waved goodbye!

My love declared in shards of ice,
"Let's build a snowman, oh, how nice!"
But he prefers to stack some flakes,
Claiming he's making winter cakes!

A snowball fight that turned quite wild,
I aimed for you, but hit a child.
We laughed and rolled in snowy clumps,
While gingerbread men hid from the thumps!

And when the evening starts to fall,
I send my heart in haikus small.
Yet one last snowman lies afar,
Winking at me—his carrot is a star!

Joyful Shadows Cast by the Moon

The moonlight spills like lemonade,
Casting shadows in a playful parade.
Snowflakes dance, just like our feet,
While reindeer glide for a late-night treat.

A snowman wearing shades so cool,
Sipping cocoa, thinking he's so fool.
We chase our shadows, hop and sway,
But trip and tumble, our plans decay!

The laughter echoes round the trees,
As squirrels laugh at our silly tease.
Our whispered secrets, soft and sweet,
The moon just giggles, can't take a seat!

What's that? A snowball flung my way?
It's cold, it's wet, but hey, I say!
With joyful hearts, we find our ground,
In moonlit glee, no frowns around!

Journey through Starry Starlings

Starlings swirl like Christmas lights,
Creating chaos in winter nights.
Off to the skies, they take their flight,
Critiquing us as we bumble by!

With cheeks aglow, we seek our dreams,
But starlings giggle, poking fun at schemes.
A glittery hat, a scarf askew,
They squawk, "You look like pudding stew!"

In silly hats, we skip and hop,
While starlings cheer, we'll never stop.
A sight like this, so soft and bright,
Turns frosty walks to pure delight!

Yet when they're gone, the world feels bare,
Snowflakes glitter, floating in air.
But wait, a snowplow rumbles loud,
To chase those starlings, a humbling crowd!

A Symphony of Smiles

A clatter of bells, a jolly sound,
As laughter bounces all around.
Clumsy dancers on the snow,
Falling over, putting on a show!

The cookies baked, a splendid mess,
A swirl of icing, what's the stress?
But when we taste, oh what delight,
One bite—then chaos, a frosted fight!

Carols sung with off-key flair,
Neighbors peek to see our fare.
With every note, a giggle shared,
Who needs a choir? We're over-prepared!

In this sweet season, fun's the aim,
As silly smiles make up the game.
So here's to laughter, love, and cheer,
A symphony for all to hear!

Illuminations of Unity

Lights are twinkling in the trees,
Neighbors fighting over cheese.
The dog steals ham, oh what a sight,
Decked out in tinsel, he's a fright!

Eggnog flows like a merry stream,
Uncle Bob's lost his Christmas dream.
Do we dance? Do we sing?
Watch out for the mistletoe sting!

Socks are filled with weird surprise,
Grandma's knitting, oh what a guise.
Every gift has a silly tag,
Wrapped up tight with a bright ol' rag!

Laughter echoes through the room,
As Dad gets stuck up in the flume.
But as we gather close and cheer,
We find the joy of being near!

A Hearth of Dreams and Aspirations

The fireplace crackles, logs in a pile,
Dad tells stories, with his usual style.
Mom's cookies burn, that's her special trick,
Santa's coming, quick! Grab a stick!

The kids are bouncing like balls on a spree,
Wishing for toys, oh won't it be free?
But just before bedtime, they hear a thud,
Is it Santa or just the neighbor's old stud?

Hot cocoa spills, oh what a mess!
Fudge on the floor? What a grim guess!
Yet we all burst into laughter so loud,
This is the best, we're all so proud!

Under the glow of lights that sparkle,
We huddle close, avoiding the quarkle.
In dreams, we'll fly on peppermint sleighs,
With giggles and joy for all of our days!

Songs of the Nativity

Carolers outside, out of tune,
Yelling 'Jingle Bells' at noon!
The cat gets scared and leaps with fright,
While Grandma tries to sing tonight.

Mittens caught in candy cane fights,
Kids' faces smeared with snowy bites.
Bells ring loud as they hit the floor,
Did someone leave the back door ajar?

Every note is a funny affair,
High pitch squeals cause wild despair.
Yet in the chaos, we all still hum,
To the goofy beat of the holiday drum!

So gather 'round, and lift your voice,
In this madness, let's all rejoice.
With laughs and jests, we'll sing and sway,
This is our side-splitting holiday!

Sparkling Serendipity

Snowflakes tumble like a playful muse,
As kids toss snowballs in bright hues.
A sled goes flying, what a thrill!
Oops! Uncle Joe, that's quite a spill!

Gifts wrapped in paper, the cats attack,
Ribbons everywhere, we can't hold back.
A squeaky toy for the pup on the run,
Now everyone's a part of the fun!

Twinkling lights on the roof so bright,
Dad attempts to hang them, what a sight!
Down he goes with a giggle and twist,
We'll say it's festive, you get the gist!

So here's to the laughter, the joy, and the cheer,
To all of the quirks that bring us near.
In this sparkly mess, let's take a bow,
With smiles and chuckles, let's celebrate now!

Glimmers of Cheer in Every Corner

Twinkling lights on the dog's tail,
A squirrel dressed up, avoiding jail.
Cookies shaped like reindeer fly,
As laughter echoes through the sky.

Snowmen dressed in winter flair,
Top hats made of cotton, full of care.
Neighbors carol with hats askew,
A festive chorus, all askew.

Mistletoe hangs from the door,
Watch out! There's Fido seeking more.
Santa's laugh can shake the walls,
While grandma breaks into wild brawls.

In every room, a silly grin,
Eggnog spills and festive din.
Happiness bounces everywhere,
Even the cat's wearing a chair!

Mirthful Memories by the Fire

Crackers pop with a mighty boom,
As Uncle Joe steals all the room.
Chestnuts roast, but not quite right,
They're more like balls of fiery fright.

Grandma knitting on her knee,
Yarns tangled like a mystery.
Kids are bouncing, shouting loud,
Santa's stuck up in a cloud.

Hot cocoa spills on the rug,
A sneaky puppy gives a shrug.
The fireplace crackles, what a sight,
As grandpa snoozes, snoring light.

Stories told with giggles shared,
Comedic tales that none have dared.
With each sip of joyous cheer,
We never want this time to clear.

A Dance of Snow and Light

Flakes of white spin round and round,
Making snow angels on the ground.
Children giggle, chasing around,
While dogs tumble, joy unbound.

Glowing orbs on branches sway,
Dancing with the night's ballet.
Snowball fights and laughter loud,
Winning trophies made of cloud.

A jolly man with a big ol' sack,
Chased by kids in a playful track.
Noses red with blissful fun,
Running under the merry sun.

As the music fills the air,
It's hard not to stop and stare.
With every twirl and hop this eve,
We know in laughter, we believe.

Enchanted by the Season's Spirit

Lights aglow on the dog's new hat,
Wobbly walks, oh, where's the mat?
Ribbons tangled in every cranny,
Our house resembles Auntie Fanny.

Sleigh bells jingle in the night,
While snowflakes dance without a fright.
Cookies vanish from the plate,
Leaving crumbs to decorate.

Cousins argue, games go wild,
Over who gets to play the child.
Cards exchanged with sneaky pranks,
With glitter scattered in the ranks.

Joy abounds in every nook,
Smiling faces, giggles, and a book.
As laughter fills the frosty air,
Warm memories linger, hearts laid bare.

A Serenade of Seasonal Grace

Jingle bells on rooftops sound,
While Santa's stuck where he's just found.
Reindeer laugh, oh what a sight,
As they eat cookies, what a bite!

Kids all giggle, tell a joke,
Mom's still searching for the yoke.
Wrapping paper, a grand mess,
Is it a gift or just more stress?

Snowmen dance with frosty cheer,
While hot cocoa melts away fear.
Christmas tunes in a silly twist,
Join the fun, you can't resist!

Cheer and laughter fill the night,
With slippers on, we take a flight.
To watch the stars from our warm place,
Warmth translates to a smiling face.

Beneath a Blanket of White

Snowflakes whisper, soft and light,
As we tumble, oh what a sight!
Falling flat on the snowy ground,
Who knew winter could be so round?

Sleds go flying, kids on a spree,
While dogs chase tails, full of glee.
Hot chocolate spills, oh what a mess,
But laughter turns frowns to success!

Frosty noses, cheeks all aglow,
While we build castles from the snow.
"More carrots!" someone calls with flair,
As the snowman raises a frozen stare.

Sipping cider, sharing tales,
Of relatives stuck in snow trails.
With playlists of songs that make us grin,
We dance around, let the fun begin!

Wishes Carried on a Crisp Breeze

Wishes flying on a brisk wind,
Santa's sleigh, a festive trend.
While kids sneak peek at what's inside,
The hope for gifts they cannot hide.

Chimneys puffing with smoke so bright,
As cookies vanish out of sight.
Elves are giggling in the shop,
Saying, "We hope your laughter won't stop!"

Mittens lost in the snowy drift,
But who needs warmth when we have gift?
A reindeer just stole our last fry,
Oh, what a prank! We wonder why.

Frosty fun, we'll play all night,
With garlands twinkling, such delight.
Until the dawn breaks in a blaze,
We'll share our joy in silly ways!

Illuminating the Darkest Hours

Lights twinkling on the tallest tree,
As cats plot mischief, oh whee!
Tinsel flying, what a surprise,
As grandpa snores with open eyes.

Underneath the mistletoe,
An awkward dance leads to 'whoa!'
Slipping, sliding, on holiday cheer,
With giggles echoing through the year.

Cousins chase each other with glee,
While grandma bakes—a mystery.
What's in her pie? A curious taste,
Believe it or not, it's a brisk race!

Even in chaos, we find our light,
In every laugh, every little fight.
Joyful moments fill the night air,
This festive season makes all hearts fair!

A Symphony of Delicate Flavors

A turkey in the oven, oh what a smell,
It wobbles and jiggles, a savory spell.
Grandma's fruitcake arrives, so brick-like it seems,
A doorstop or dessert? It's up to your dreams.

Cookies in dishes, all merry and bright,
We nibble and giggle, in pure delight.
The eggnog is spiked, with a rumble so strong,
One sip too many and we sing the wrong song.

Mashed potatoes overflowing, a buttery sea,
A brawl for the gravy, oh let there be glee!
Uncles debating where the ham should go,
While Aunties just whisper, "Will he ever know?"

At the end of the day, oh what a feast,
With leftovers aplenty, our laughing won't cease.
The flavors collide, in a joyful array,
So here's to the trying, as we roll on the hay.

Graced by the Season's Gifts

Presents piled high, what a sight to behold,
Wrapping paper flying, as stories unfold.
A cat in the corner, it pounces with zest,
On ribbons and bows, it's simply the best.

The tree is adorned with tinsel and cheer,
Little ones whispering, "Is Santa still here?"
A sock on the shelf for our furry friend,
With treats just for him, his winter may mend.

Laughter erupts in a gift-opening spree,
Uncle Bob's old sweater, quite a sight to see.
"Wear it with pride!" is the jovial tone,
But watch out for mothballs, they're aiming to drone.

In a flurry of wishes, we hold onto glee,
Forgetfulness reigns, but we'll always agree.
With laughter and joy, the presents unwrapped,
This season of giving, we're happily trapped.

Threads of Tradition Weave Love

The ornaments hang, each one tells a tale,
Of triumphs and fails, oh the joy, oh the wail.
A knitted sweater passed through many a year,
With a hole in the sleeve, but we hold it so dear.

Carols sung loud in a comical pitch,
While Grandpa sneezes, and starts to twitch.
Mistletoe hangs, but nobody's keen,
Unless it's for donuts, oh what a scene!

Games by the fire, with a twist and a shout,
Watch out for that cousin, he's turning about.
The stories get taller with every round,
As we roll on the floor, laughter's the sound.

Traditions are quirky, they tug at our heart,
Through strange family ties, we'll never part.
With all of our laughter, and memories bright,
We weave love through the laughter, a holiday light.

Radiant Smiles in the Chill

Snowflakes descend with a frosty twist,
Building snowmen so round, they can't be missed.
The scarves are too long, and the mittens, a joke,
While we chase our own shadows, and laugh till we croak.

Sledding down hills, with a whoop and a glide,
Flipping and flopping, we tumble, we slide.
"Watch out for ice!" is the call in the air,
But who really listens? We just don't care!

Hot cocoa awaits, with marshmallows galore,
With giddy excitement, we slurp, we implore.
As gingerbread houses melt away in a heap,
All part of the fun, it's not meant to keep.

So gather 'round close, as the night starts to fall,
With glow sticks and laughter, we welcome them all.
Through the chill of the season, we'll find a good cheer,
With radiant smiles, we'll spread warmth far and near.

Harmony in a Starry Sky

Under twinkling lights, we dance so free,
A turkey in the oven - oh, what a spree!
Uncle Fred's mad jokes, they fly like snow,
While Aunt May tries to keep up with the flow.

Hot cocoa spills as we cheerfully sing,
A chorus of chaos that only joy can bring.
The tree stands tall, with glittering flair,
As we dodge the cat, who's now hiding somewhere.

Laughter echoes, the snowflakes do twirl,
With popcorn garlands that start to unfurl.
A misfit of moments, all wrapped up in cheer,
Making memories, 'tis the season, we hear!

Mismatched socks, and hats all askew,
As we snicker and giggle like kids on the loo.
In this festive frenzy, we shine and we glow,
With sprinkles of mischief, we steal the show!

The Light of Togetherness

Gather round the table, what a massive feast,
The pet cat's eyeing the ham, the sneaky beast!
With grandma's secret recipe, all smeared in goo,
It's a culinary chaos that none can undo.

Popcorn in the microwave, starting to blast,
While the dog's plotting to eat it real fast.
Siblings throwing snowballs, some hits and some misses,
All bundled up tight, with laughter and kisses.

A snowman's built, but collapsed in a pile,
His carrot nose waving with a half-hearted smile.
Tinsel that tangles, and lights that don't shine,
Yet we're all decked out, feeling truly divine!

Around us the jingle of bells fills the air,
Grandpa snores loudly, without any care.
Though things go awry, we cherish this mess,
In the warmth of our love, we are truly blessed.

Hidden Blessings in the Cold

Chillin' by the fire, hot cider in hand,
With marshmallows melting, oh, isn't it grand?
A squirrel in the tree, with quite the appetite,
Grabs a bauble, dashes - what a comical sight!

Scarves wrapped too tight, in a snowy jam,
While Billy's buildup of snowballs is quite the plan.
A slip on the ice leads to giggles and grins,
As we brush off the snow and give it another spin.

Our wish lists forgotten, they're lost in the fun,
As we play in the snow, racing everyone!
And though it gets chilly, our hearts are aglow,
The warmth of our friendship is all that we know.

So let us embrace every chuckle and cheer,
As we revel together, this time of the year.
Though frosty outside, our spirits take flight,
We find joy in the laughter that sparkles so bright!

Embracing the Spirit of Giving

Boxes of trinkets, piled high to the brim,
All ready for wrapping, each sparkly whim.
A game of who's got the best secret gift,
But Dad buys socks, which gives us all a rift.

"Surprise!" when it's opened, and oops, it's a book,
That's destined to collect dust, just take a look!
With ribbons gone wild, and tape stuck in hair,
We're all in a tangle, but we're not in despair.

Gift cards and gadgets, we trade and we swap,
While the dog runs off with that shiny top prop.
Oh, the joy of the season, so wacky and bright,
As we giggle and grin, under stars shining light.

Though giving's the point, it's the laughter we treasure,
With moments like these, we find lasting pleasure.
So come raise a cheer, for it's more than a prize,
It's the joy shared together that truly supplies!

Whispers of Winter's Embrace

Snowflakes dance, it's quite absurd,
They coat my nose, oh how it stirred!
A shiver here, a giggle there,
The winter's chill gives quite the scare.

Hot cocoa spills, it stains my shirt,
My friends all laugh, oh what a flirt!
We build a snowman, a lopsided sight,
His carrot nose gives quite a fright.

Outside it's cold, but here's the trick,
We blast some tunes, and do a quick jig!
We flail our arms, we stomp our feet,
Oh what a sight, isn't this neat?

So here's to winter, the frosty fun,
With laughter shared, we come undone!
A cozy night, let's dance and play,
In this chilly glow, we'll laugh away!

Flickering Lights of Hope

Lights are strung, a tangled ball,
We trip and giggle, oh what a fall!
The cat takes chase, a wild-eyed race,
As we wrestle him, we find our place.

Cookies baking, a sugary mess,
Flour on noses, we must confess!
With sprinkles flying, sugar fights,
Our kitchen chaos, oh what delights!

Stockings hung, but with caution,
For sneaky pets, they're pure inaction!
Presents wrapped, they look quite sly,
Oh no! That one just caught my eye!

We toast with mugs, our cheer fills the room,
The laughter rolls like a fragrant bloom.
So let's be silly, let's dance all night,
With hearts aglow, everything feels right!

A Hearth's Warm Embrace

The fire crackles, it pops with glee,
We roast marshmallows, oh so free!
Sticky fingers, a gooey delight,
As we share stories in the night.

Sweaters on, they're two sizes too big,
We laugh together, do a little jig!
The old dog snores, he steals the show,
While we plot more mischief, with hot cocoa flow.

Holiday movies, with laughter and cheer,
We shout at the screen, "Oh dear, oh dear!"
Popcorn flings, we create our mess,
But in this chaos, we feel truly blessed.

So gather round, let stories spin,
For every tale, we join in a grin.
With heartwarming warmth, we find our place,
In this crazy world, we embrace the grace!

Echoes of Joyful Laughter

Jingle bells ring, but out of tune,
We laugh so hard, we might take a swoon!
Dancing in circles, an awkward spree,
Oh look at Uncle, he's lost his key!

The kids run wild, like little sprites,
Throwing glitter, oh what a sight!
A hiccup here, a snort over there,
We gather the joy, like confetti in the air.

With cocoa smeared, and smiles so wide,
We race each other, on a laugh-filled ride.
Snowballs tossed, they hit the mark,
Creating laughter, like fireflies in the dark.

These echoes ring, through frosty nights,
In every giggle, our spirit ignites.
So here's to fun, to silliness rare,
In this bright season, we find love to share!